ALEXANDER GLAZUNOV

CONCERTO Nº 1

IN F MINOR

FOR

PIANO AND ORCHESTRA

OP. 92

3078

SUGGESTIONS FOR USING THIS MMO EDITION

WE HAVE TRIED to create a product that will provide you an easy way to learn and perform a concerto with a full orchestra in the comfort of your own home. Because it involves a fixed orchestral performance, there is an inherent lack of flexibility in tempo and cadenza length. The following MMO features and techniques will reduce these inflexibilities and help you maximize the effectiveness of the MMO practice and performance system:

Where the soloist begins a movement *solo*, we have provided an introductory measure with subtle taps inserted at the actual tempo before the soloist's entrance.

Chapter stops on your CD are conveniently located throughout the piece at the beginnings of practice sections, and are cross-referenced in the score. This should help you quickly find a desired place in the music as you learn the piece.

Chapter stops have also been placed at orchestra entrances (after cadenzas, for example) so that, with the help of a second person, it is possible to perform a seamless version of the concerto alongside your MMO CD accompaniment. While we have allotted what is generally considered an average amount of time for a cadenza, each performer will have a different interpretation and observe individual tempi.

Your personal rendition may preclude a perfect "fit" within the space provided. Therefore, by having a second person press the pause ❚❚ button on your CD player after the start of each cadenza, followed by the next track ▶▶❙ button, your CD will be cued to the orchestra's re-entry. When you as soloist are at the end of the cadenza or other solo passage, the second person can press the play ▶ (or pause ❚❚ button) on the CD remote to allow a synchronized orchestra re-entry.

Regarding tempi: we have observed generally accepted tempi, but some may wish to perform at a different tempo, or to slow down or speed up the accompaniment for practice purposes. You can purchase from mmo (or from other audio and electronics dealers) specialized CD players which allow variable speed while maintaining proper pitch. This is an indispensable tool for the serious musician and you may wish to look into purchasing this useful piece of equipment for full enjoyment of all your MMO editions.

We want to provide you with the most useful practice and performance accompaniments possible. If you have any suggestions for improving the MMO system, please feel free to contact us. You can reach us by e-mail at info@musicminusone.com.

Music Minus One

3078

ALEXANDER GLAZUNOV

CONCERTO № 1
IN F MINOR
FOR
PIANO AND ORCHESTRA
OP. 92

Glazunov's Piano concerto No 1 in F minor, op. 92

ALEXANDER KONSTANTINOVICH GLAZUNOV was born 10 August 1865 in St. Petersburg, Russia, to two talented musicians: His mother was a near-professional pianist, and his father was a sophisticated amateur violinist. His musical initiation started at a young age, for by the age of six he had begun studying piano. Shortly thereafter he began studying viola and violoncello, largely so he could accompany his parents in playing chamber music.

The young Glazunov began serious piano study at age twelve with Nikolai Elenkovsky, who had taught Glazunov's mother. A year later Elenkovsky left St. Petersburg and Glazunov's mother sought advice over her son's future. She turned to the famous composer Mili Balakirev, who immediately recognized Alexander's impressive musical gifts—including composition—and matched the young boy with Nikolai Rimsky-Korsakov.

Glazunov began studies with Rimsky-Korsakov almost immediately, and two years later Balakirev conducted the première of the sixteen-year-old's First Symphony. The acclaim which followed was tremendous. The great Franz Liszt arranged the symphony's first performance outside Russia, in Weimar, and predicted a tremendous career for the boy. By twenty-one years of age, Glazunov was hailed throughout Europe as one of the great musical beacons on the horizon and one of Russia's foremost composers.

Glazunov's talents for composing began to blossom in a wealth of new works: his symphonic tone-poems, such as *Stenka Rasine,* showed his originality and his fascination with the exotic and the fantastic. Glazunov was heavily influenced by Liszt's experimentation in depicting nature through music, and he had a fertile imagination that, in combination with his keen ear and mastery of orchestral texture, could create something of extraordinarily unique beauty.

In 1899 he became a professor at the St. Petersburg Conservatory and found he had a powerful affinity for teaching, which was borne out in his being appointed director of the Conservatory in 1905. It was in his position here that Glazunov possibly made his greatest contribution to music, aside from his own compositions. During his tenure, he persuaded the young Sergei Prokofiev's parents to allow him to pursue composition rather than the engineering future they envisioned for their son. Among Glazunov's most famous students were Igor Stravinsky, Dmitri Tiomkin, and Dmitri Shostakovich. All his students were nothing short of reverential toward their master and overwhelmingly agreed on the enormous influence he had on their work. So revered was he that he would endure in his position at the conservatory through the throes of revolution; it wasn't until 1928 that he used the excuse of poor health to quietly resign and relocate to Paris.

Glazunov composed a huge body of work in all genres. In addition to his huge orchestral output, he became fascinated with the ballet; his *Raymonda* and *The Seasons* are classics to this day. One of the greatest strengths of Glazunov's music is that is serves as a bridge between Russian and Western musical styles. His command of orchestration and his amazing melodic sense gave him innate tools to appeal to a wide audience, and he succeeded for decades—even if he was criticized late in life for not changing with the times.

Despite such criticisms, Glazunov continued to explore new territory, and one of his most memorable experiments came from his exposure to Jazz and his fascination with the saxophone. In 1934, two years before his death at seventy, Glazunov premiered his Saxophone Concerto†, which remains one of the classics of the repertoire for that instrument.

Glazunov's first instrument was the piano, but because he never completed a full course of instruction he always deprecated his mastery of the instrument from a performance standpoint. Nevertheless, he was to write a large amount of music for the instrument. In 1889, he began work on a piano concerto, but put it aside the next year. Not until twenty years later, in 1910, did he push himself to finish what he had begun as a youth. He had set before himself many compositional challenges in the structure of the work, and on 21 June 1910 he wrote to pianist Konstantin Igumnov:

> After arriving at the dacha, the first thing I turned to was finishing the concerto. Only the piano portions remain, but I'm encountering every obstacle possible: I have constant doubt over what to assign to the piano and what to give the orchestra. And though I understand the piano, I am still unschooled in it, and what is comfortable for me may not be practical to an expert pianist and vice-versa. I'm given comfort in that [Leopold] Godowsky, to whom I gave my sketches, didn't have many comments. And in working out certain piano portions I feel that I've made some progress in technique myself. I will not yet orchestrate the concerto, but will attempt to finish the solo part, which I will send you in sections after 1 July.

Though dedicated to Godowsky, the concerto finally saw the light of day with Igumnov at the keyboard in the Hall of Nobility on 24 February 1912, with Glazunov at the podium. It was enthusiastically received and was published shortly thereafter by Belaiev.

The concerto is set in two parts; the first begins with a sombre *Allegro moderato* theme cast in a rich orchestral palette which is quintessential Glazunov. The piano then enters solo with a thickly Lisztian bravura flourish; this gives way to the sensuous, beautiful main theme. The pianism is so rich and orchestral in texture it comes as a surprise when the orchestra reenters, bringing the theme to a throbbing, lush climax. The interplay of orchestra and piano throughout the rest of the movement is brilliantly conceived and creates a thrilling experience.

The second movement is cast in a theme-and-variations plan. The initial theme is rich and sweetly melancholy, and Glazunov gives it a melt-in-your-mouth orchestral setting. The variations are somewhat reminiscent of Glazunov's *Theme and Variations* for solo piano, op. 73, and there are hints of sympathy for Cesar Franck's *Variations Symphoniques*. But Glazunov is able to meld this massive set of nine variations into a drama unto itself, brilliantly using contrasts between variations. He also calls upon his love for the ballet, for which the entire piece shows an affinity. In the final variation Glazunov ingeniously recalls the first movement; and through clever manipulation of tempo, and by giving the impression of a constant upward rise of tonality, he creates a joyous and truly exhilarating finale.

Glazunov's works went through a rough time critically through the middle of the twentieth century, when many of his more atonally directed students grabbed the spotlight. But it can't be said that Glazunov was completely ignored in Western Europe and the Americas, as his ballets and symphonies held on tenaciously. It is refreshing to know that his work finds a more sympathetic audience at the dawn of the twenty-first century, where it is seeing the light of day once again. Here is a composer who rarely fails to please, and his First Piano Concerto is undeniable proof of that fact.

–Douglas Scharmann

---

†Glazunov's Saxophone Concerto is also available from Music Minus One (catalogue number MMO CD 4132).

A Monsieur Leopold Godowsky
hommage respectueux de l'auteur

CONCERTO № 1
FOR PIANO & ORCHESTRA, OP. 92

Alexander Glazunov
(1865-1936)

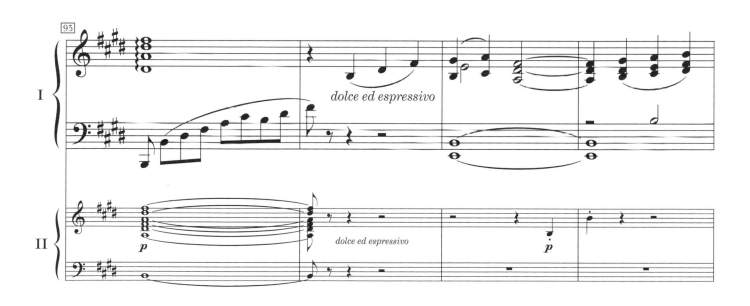

II.
Tema con variazioni

Variation V (Intermezzo)

(Two taps precede music) Allegro (♪ = **152**)

Variation VI (Quasi una fantasia)

Variation VII (Mazurka)

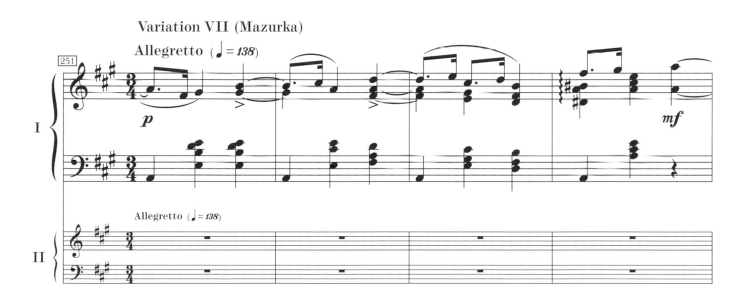

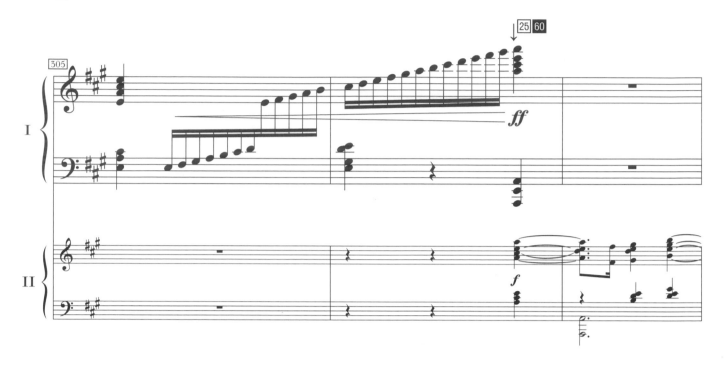

Variation VIII (Scherzo)
Allegro ma non troppo (♩ = 96)

Cadenza *Piano solo*

Variation IX (Finale)

Allegro moderato (♩ = *104*)

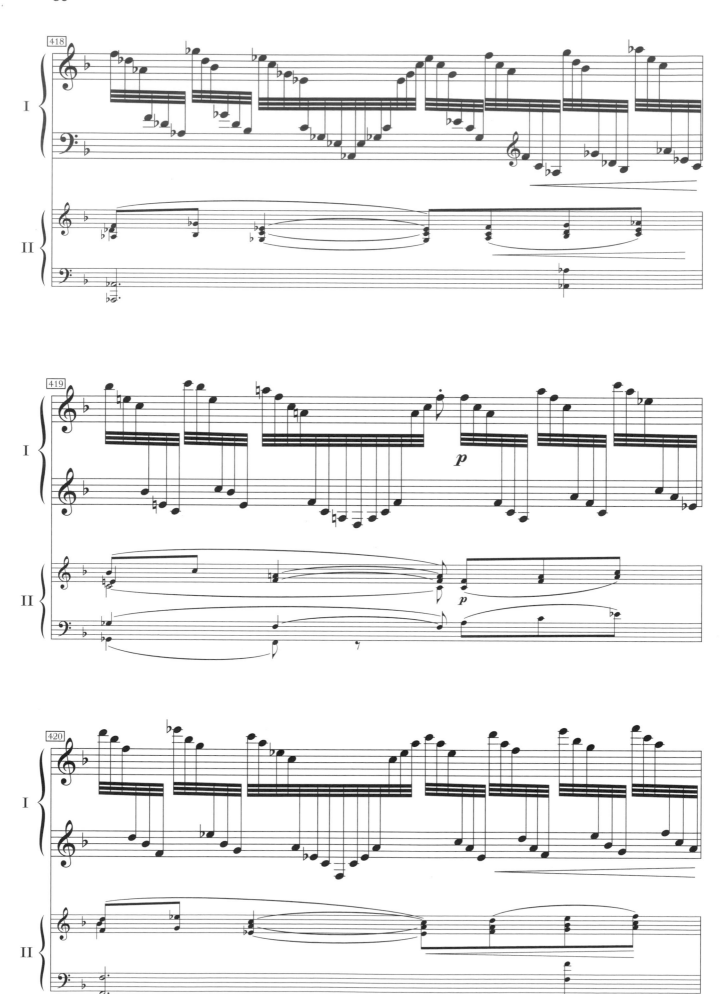

animando poco a poco

MUSIC MINUS ONE
50 Executive Boulevard
Elmsford, New York 10523-1325
800-669-7464 (U.S.)/914-592-1188 (International)

www.musicminusone.com
e-mail: mmogroup@musicminusone.com

MMO 3078